Loveology

A Soliloquy of a Man's Heart

CLAUDE GARRETSON

WWW.CLAUDEGARRETSON.COM

EDITED BY
Terry-Michele Lucas
Nadine Geddes

Cover Designed
Claude Garretson

Literary Management
I Had a Happy Production

First published by Dog Ear Publishing
4011 Vincennes Rd
Indianapolis, IN 46268
www.dogearpublishing.net

ISBN: 978-1-4575-4409-5

This book is printed on acid-free paper.

Printed in the United States of America

To Michelle,

My sweet, sexy, friend, I hope you find these poems, earthy, spicy, and stimulating. May these words serve as an aphrodisiacal appetizer that arouses your appetite for a salacious, romantic moment of pleasure.

Much love,

CG

For all the women whom I loved and who loved me.

Scenes of Love

Scene 1: Pursuit ....Page 1

Scene 2: Romance ....Page 17

Scene 3: Eroticism ....Page 41

Scene 4: Break Up ....Page 71

Scene 5: The End ....Page 95

Scene 6: You Can Still Smile ....Page 101

Encore ....Page 109

Pursuit

THE GLOW OF YOU

The pursuit of something beyond myself,
So real I felt its presence
 though I had not possessed it.
I search the heavens.
Galaxies upon galaxies.
Like the light of the moon in the night
        comes not from itself
        but from something greater.

Stars edging one another
 upon the crest of the evening tide.
I grasped and held One
I thought it was You.

A mirage.
A Light with no warmth.
A flicker with no flame.
Somewhere it died.
        I know not when nor where.

Yesterday's reality
        Sleeps with today's memory
Darkness in the heart
        shields Heaven's light from the eyes.

Somewhere beyond my world,
        Abides one for me.
        A precious gift from
        the giver and taker.
I know not where
        and I know not when
        But I shall find You.

And when I do

Ra will rise,
inspiring Aurora
with a kiss and
They will dance the Darkness away.

And the lies of the Lunar light
in the midnight sky
will succumb to the truth of its origination.

When I find You

Heavenly bodies will rejoice
in the essence of their beauty
Saturn will submit its Ring to
Venus
Consummating their eternal oneness.

When I find You

Each rising of the Sun
will give us a virgin day
untouched by yesterday.

When I find You

You and I will see the Light
of Heaven's Candle burning forever.

When I find You

You will be at the center
of Everything that revolves.

When I find You

The Glow Of You
will be a reflection throughout
the Universe.

I know not where
I know not when
But I will find You.

ANGEL

Somewhere in heaven God is watching me
And he knows my needs.
He sent His angel
And His angel appeared before my eyes
In the form of you.

HOW BEAUTIFUL ARE YOU?

You are beautiful.

How beautiful?
Too picturesque for words.

If the world were as beautiful as you,
there would be peace throughout the land.
Hunger would not be known.

How beautiful?
Unmarked as a new born child,
Vibrant as a Pacific coral reef.

How beautiful?
Fresh as a budding perennial flower.
Perfect as a glorious sunrise.
Luminous as Sirius[1].

How beautiful?
Sophisticated as Eroica[2]
Yet simple as the word "yes".

I am
in awe of your beauty.

Wondering why I am so fortunate
to experience your loveliness
with every sense of my Self.
To see, smell, feel, hear, taste
your exquisiteness
is absolutely wonderful!

---

[1] Brightest star seen from earth.
[2] Beethoven's Symphony No. 3 in E Flat Major considered one of the most complicated symphonies.

How beautiful?
Too beautiful for this poem to express.

So I will just say,
You are quite gorgeous!

IT'S YOUR SHOW

If love was a motion picture,
My attention would be captured.
In the starring role would be you,
Patiently, I wait for my cue.

Just to audition as your leading man,
Surely, I am your most faithful fan.
When casting time is near,
Rest assure I would appear.

There is no need for me to rehearse my part.
Because, my role comes from the heart.
Wishing to be your everlasting hero,
Honey, you are the star of the show.

The picture plays over and over in my mind,
It turns out to be a dream each and every time.
If it was only true,
The Oscar would go to you.

If love was a movie,
The world would be
Our audience and they know it to be true,
Just how much I adore you.

I'd turn down the Academy Award.
It is you I want as my reward.
You received the Oscar for perfection.
Baby, you have no competition

Lines forming from here to eternity,
People coming from all over to see.
A performance never before seen,
As we dance across the screen.

The picture plays over and over in my mind,
It turns out to be a dream every time.
If it was only true,
The Oscar would surely go to you.

I'd give my heart and soul to star in your show,
Baby, my happiness and joy to you I owe.

SPEAK OF YOU

Speak
to me.
Whisper gently in my ear.
Intimately articulate
your thoughts.
I want to hear
everything there is about you.
Come closer to me.
There is more to you than the eyes see.
Speak.
Tenderly massage your voice
upon the canvas of my flesh.
Paint a portrait of the Heavens
with words of you.
Your magnificence is divine.
So
Speak.
I plead for you to
share yourself with me
in this moment.
For I'm overwhelmed by my hunger
to know more of you
than the rest.
Submissively I wait for you to
Speak.
Express yourself
through your walls
of hesitation.
Open yourself
and
I shall come inside.
Beloved, the rhythm of you
vibrates within my Soul.
I dance across the clouds
so I can hear the Heavens.

Speak
of you.
I am here for you,
my heart listens
for you to
Speak.

WE'VE MET...

You my dear asked if we have met. Don't you remember?

When you lie asleep in the twilight hour, I tiptoed through your dreams, penetrated your mind and stroked your every thought of me. I am your most pleasant nightmare. Awakening you night after night in a hot sweat, when I caressed your dreams, touched your heart and massaged your soul.

When the night falls and darkness encases your outer being, I yield a shaft of light into your spirit and you radiate with the glow of satisfaction.

When your heart drowns in an ocean of loneliness, I remove the wet from the water. Romancing you across the Seven Seas under a blanket of glimmering stars, on a backdrop of pure blackness. Placing your body upon the shores of ecstasy, leaving an imprint in the sands of time.

Oh yes we've met! Oh don't you remember?

When your hopes of love are smothered, I render a gasp of pure intoxicating emotion and my love would touch the intangible.

When I look into your eyes, read your mind and in the midst of your thoughts there I am, holding you in my arms. Protecting your nature from nature itself.

When you fantasize of a Knight in Shining Armor, I appear with Armor in the Night. Whisk you away on a black stallion named Passion and we would ride and ride until the sun would rise. . .

And when the morning dew moistens your daydreams, freeing your mind to wander to foreign lands and unknown places, searching for fulfillment and each time, you find me.

When my love rose and took you to Heaven's gates and you responded as if you met the Divine Creator and Venus the God of Love looked upon us and took notes.

And yet you ask if we've met. Oh yes we've met and you remember!

NEVER FORGET HER

I'll never forget her.

Her sweet, mocha chocolate complexion. An Elixir. My eyes had the pleasure of tasting her beauty; Intoxication.

My nose could hear her fragrance swirling, twirling,
within the wind. Mesmerized? Slightly, I guess.

I had to say something to her.

When I tried, the poetic verse that once was, abandoned me
like the night, abandons the morning at sunrise.

One moment it's there, then it's gone.

Instead of reciting
Hughes,
    Hayden,
    or Baldwin

my words went something like this:

"You're so fine,

I'd stick you to the roof
    of my mouth like
    Jiffy on a Ritz.

I'd licked until you were 5 pounds lighter
    and two shades brighter.

Flip you like a flapjack.

You're the One
    that makes a zero
    a Ten.

Sweeter than
        Project Kool-Aid.

Prettier than a
        Coupe-DeVille on Father's Day.

Baby you're fine.

Eat you like an Oreo cookie,
eat the cream in between
saving your chocolate sides for last.

You make me kinkier
than a nappy afro. "

Embarrassed? Absolutely!

She looked me up and down as if I was about to be thoroughly "read" like a Sunday newspaper. Her eyes roll more than a pair of Las Vegas dice and her neck starting popping and shifting as if she was trying to get it in gear.

Before I could apologize she started.

"If you were a real man,
you eat me like your mama's cooking;
faithfully each day and several times on Sunday.

I'd be your coffee in the morning,
get you up and going.

Suck you like a jaw-breaker,
all day long.

If you were a real man,
you be more like Nike
and Just Do It."

Romance

Oh what darkness, when the moon joins the sun.
A task to distinguish between day and night.
Yet when love joins two into one,
There renders Heaven's light.

THE ART OF LOVE

Love is the art of one's inner being,
And only a true artist of love.
Can create passion in another
with the stroke of an emotion.

And you my dear
possess my last piece of love.
Sculpted to meet the perfection of the possessor,
Designed especially with you in my mind.

With your heart as my canvas
I sketched a painting of devotion.
With your beauty as my model,
I molded a statue of splendor.

A collage of my memories
harmonize into an eternal portrait of you.

Many seek to have such a creation.
Making what I have given you, so precious and valuable.
A masterpiece of perfection,
An Original,
So unique, so you.

I bequeath to you,
with all my dedication
This one and only,
This masterpiece known
under the Heavens
as The Art Of Love.

A PLACE

Somewhere there is a place

where
The heavens touch the earth
rendering a stage for
an orchestra of stars to compose a radiant rhapsody
that ignites one's true self.

where
Tomorrow and today are one,
a reflection of yesterday.

where
The mind relinquishes all to the heart
and the imagination is just and image of what is real.

where
Infinity is not long enough
and forever becomes forever and a day.

where
All is born and nothing dies.

where
Burning desires are more
than eternal flames of passion
that warms one's lust to . . .

where
You seek to be, but are afraid to venture
for those before me
have proclaimed to have taken you there . . .

where
You desire to be more than you
but to be me and I, you.

A place where we are one.
One and only one.

where
The only request is for you to
close your eyes and
open your heart
and
I will take you to this place

where
I have waited for your arrival.
A place
where
I call . . . LOVE.

IF I WERE. . . THEN I WOULD

If I were an artist,
I would paint a mural of you
        across the highest mountains,
or maybe a composer,
        then I would write a symphony to you for
        the birds to sing in the spring.
If I were a writer
        there would be libraries
        full of novels about you,
or if maybe a voyager,
        then I would travel to the end of the universe
searching for you.
Since I'm none of those,
I'll place a kiss upon you,
        tell you that I love you
        and that
If I were . . . then I would. . .

THE EDGE OF THE OASIS

I remember that day:

I danced
the edge of
the oasis,

Wading
gently along
the
coastal shore.

Occasionally,
Moisture
from nature's pool
sprayed my face
as the gushing waves
came
and
poured
over onto
the bordering
sandy skin.

Solicited by
the wetness
to submerge myself

head first,
instead
I just admired
the symmetry.

Deep, deep waters
flowed
so close,
nothing but

a hairline
separated the shore
from the unsure.

I wanted to be nowhere but where
I was.

Conceivably bathing
myself
in heaven and earth.

The thought
is poetic.

Warmth browsed
my entire surface.

Soothing. . .

The sun
was radiant.

oh it
was
a pleasant and memorable day.

I'd love to tread the edge of the oasis again. . .

NOT ENOUGH TIME

If I could live forever,
longer than infinity magnified by infinity,
it would not be long enough.
It is nothing more
          than a grain of sand
          in the
          Sahara's hourglass.

          I need all the grains,
          each one representing infinite time
          to be with you.

As I sit here
          and admire your beauty,
I realize that it transcends
all dimensions of time.
Making me forget the past,
          desire the future
          and cherish and I do mean cherish
          this present moment with you.

Look out the window,
notice the city skyline
in the night.
Observe the bed
          of white lights
but there
          over there
          is one
purplish blue
          light.
You can't help but
          notice it lying on
          that white bed of lights.

You are that purplish blue light
          shining . . . some say
          purple is the color of love
and some say
blue is the color of royalty
Majestic Amour. . .

My one wish
is to sit next
to you
on that pedestal
on which you reside.

There are
no diamonds
shimmering to a band of gold
on your hand.

Forgive me but
somewhere,
someone
would be honored
to place the
circle of life
upon your precious finger.

We can begin
          searching
for that person
          tonight.
Look out at that skyline
          and
stay with me,
          don't say yes
and
          don't say no,

just be
	and let's
watch each
	light disappear
until you
are the
	only thing
shining.
A night
	is not
	enough time,
but it's
	the beginning to forever.

THE LOVE I HAVE

I love
your hair, how it

flows with the
gentlest breeze and
stands still against the
strongest winds.

I love how it covers
your head,

filled with the thoughts from
the greatest philosophers
and rhythms from
the corner symphonies.

I Love how it sits erect upon
your body,

so elegant, and
graceful with the
comfort only your
robust features could bestow.

I LOve how it is encompassed by
your skin,

as dark as a
southern night and
as golden as the
morning sun.

I LOVe how it accentuates
your lips,

delicate to

speak soft words and
strong to
speak your thoughts.

I LOVE how you vary,

forever different.

I LOVE YOU As My
wife
mother
daughter
sister
friend.
I LOVE YOU AS A
WOMAN!

SUN GODDESS

A Sun Goddess
that's who you
are.
I
earth's green pasture
lying beneath
        you.

Morning you rise.
        I wake
        and blossom.

Midday
        you peak,

my olive blades
        respond
        with erect posture.

Dusk arrives
        and you
        slowly subside.

Night
        f
        a
        l
        l
        s

        and
        you disappear,

but I know
you're there
I feel your presence,
your warmth,
illuminates
the twilight
heavens.

LOVE MEMORIES

January

There was a mild snow flurry.
Winds played a romantic melody.
There you were, snuggled next to me.
Oh how precious love can be.

February

Permanently etched in my memory,
Are special moments, so extraordinary.
Filled with unforgettable ecstasy.
Winds are now playing a full rhapsody.

March

One brisk day in the park.
We left an everlasting mark.
Under a rainbow, a radiant arch.
Glisten intense love sparks.

April

The spring air was still.
The world seemed to be at our will.
We experienced love's thrill.
To an audience of daffodils.

May

It was a passionately warm day.
Nature gave us warm green grass to lay.
Over and over the wind would gently say,
"Forever together, never shall you stray."

June

One night we gazed at a full moon.
Stars danced to a poetic tune.
The morning sun came, climaxing at noon.
Moisture dripping. Night would return soon.

July

One day the clouds would cry.
Sending tears of joy from the sky.
Heaven liberated a gentle sigh.
Bestowing happiness upon you and I.

August

The summer sun beamed down on us.
We spent the day feeling anxious.
We spoke about commitment and trust.
Realizing that our love was just.

September

I so vividly remember,
When I asked, "Is there anyone better?"
The leaves rustled a soothing whisper.
"No there is not", was the answer.

October

Darkness grew and daylight became shorter,
As temperatures subsided, feeling cooler.
Dreamy nocturnal moments seem cozier.
Those moments with you, were a pleasure.

November

The wind blew causing the leaves to gather.
Nothing but you seemed to matter.
From your love, I shall never recover.
No one else could make me happier.

December

The season has changed to winter.
My love to you, I will render.
I promise to always be tender.
For you are a gift from the Creator.

MY UNIVERSE

You are my universe.
I wish to travel to the edge of you,
exploring your extremities.
Venturing into every Black Hole.

Yes, you are my universe.
To frolic with the stars,
in your eyes,
under a black canopy.

A midnight sanctuary. . .

The sun never sets
in your presence

yet there is
an eternal darkness
that you possess.

Such diversity beholds beauty.

Your vastness thrills me,
incites me
to endeavor to experience all of you.
But my lifetime
is bounded.
To live forever
in multiples of infinity,
then maybe
I could. . .

You are my universe,
The Beginning,
The End,
and
the Life between.

NATURE OF LOVE

Warmer than the rays from the sun,
Gentler than the summer air.
My heart and soul are now one.
Since having your love near.

Greater than any ocean or sea,
That embraces the sand upon the shore.
The love you give to me,
I could not ask for more.

VACATION?

The morning I arrived,
noticing your bags packed.
I remember that feeling,
Thinking you were never coming back.

Though you were only
leaving for 4 days or more.
I hated to see you
walk out that door.

Your plane landed
on or about two.
That's when I really
began missing you.

The first night,
was the worst.
Loneliness, depression,
I've been cursed.

This is the first time
we've been apart.
Still doesn't help
to soothe my broken heart.

Several times I may
call you on the phone.
Just to ease the pain
of being alone.

I listen to Marvin
"Let's Get It On"
Just torturing myself
while you're gone.

You'll soon be home,
That I realized.
Everyone can tell,
By the sparkle in my eyes.

Now as you read this,
I am no longer blue.
You have returned home,
I truly missed you.

MISSING YOU

Sensual, sexy and seductive. The limitation of the language has been reached for these are but gentle describers of an experience that shall never be replicated other than my memory repeating itself. Each encounter with you has a signature of its own . . .each interlude with you transcends the boundaries of my imagination . . .each rendezvous with you expands my basic wants, desires and needs . . .only for them to condense to the simple want, desire and need for you.

Your fragrance lingers waiting to dance with the air that I breathe. A silhouette lies here next to me; an imprint of your precious frame that I held tightly. It's, as if you never left, yet I know you're gone. It may only be for a short moment but short moments are eternity's clone when you are absent. I listen and I can hear the hands on the clock trying to pull me closer to that moment when you will return to your rightful place. Tic...Toc...Tic...Toc. I've learned that the best weapon against loneliness is fond memories. So when loneliness tries to creep into my life I just think of you. I must confess it's not the same as having you in the flesh.

Daylight is tapping at the window; I think its wants my company. I must take this moment to chaperon the Sun as it rises. I see its warmth radiating across the morning sky. Slowly moving. You notice that when it reaches Heaven's center the calmness of its warmth is aroused. The rays reach to Heaven's ends and everything feels its burning passionate embrace. For within a Day's life the Sun will have come and gone but for that brief moment when the Sun is at its peak, the Day is luminous . . . with love. As the Sun transverses the remainder of its arc there is no doubt that the Day is a different Day.

I am that Day and you are my Sun.

Until the short moments become past moments and you are in my arms again, I will leave these words for you to remember:

Amor vincit omnia et nos cedamus amori.

(Love conquers all and let us yield to it [Love])

HONEYMOON

I've taken a wife.
Forever changing my life.
The change may be soon
I missed the plane for the honeymoon!

Eroticism

Place your love on a plate
I will endlessly dine.
Place your heart upon me.
I will give you mine.

SHOWERS...OF LOVE

Droplets of rain
From the sky above,
Moisture upon your lips,
Wetness from your love

caress my body
engulf me whole.
Make me scream,
make me BOLD.

Hold me close,
take me in.
Beads of sweat
stimulate my skin

Open gently,
open wide.
Feel the warmth
deep inside.

Pull me in,
push me out.
Make me moan,
make me shout.

Upon the sill,
Listen to the rain.
Together we are,
together we came

Embrace me gently,
yet with might.
Love me forever,
more than the night.

I want to stay
but I must go
I need not explain,
I think you know.

There is no other,
for you are the best.
I have given you
the ultimate test.

Listen to rain,
hear it dance.
I have finally found
TRUE romance.

VOLCANO

My Love boils,
the fire is hot.
You feel the uncontrollable
eruption
as it explodes inside of you.
Your body shivers
with feverish trembles.
Tremors
part your limbs
and
your volcano of love
explodes
and gushes.
Fiery streams
meander along the curves
of your inner thighs.
I furnish a tongue
to dam the flood.
A mouthful of love
is brought back to you.
And the volcanic passions
are simmered
with a cool kiss.

UNCHARTERED

Let me put you at ease.

Listen to the music
    in the background.
    Notice
    how the collaboration of notes
    form a solitary serenade of the musician's
    ambitions.

Relax,
    Allow yourself to release
    those repressed
    feelings or
    should I refer to them
    as cravings.
    The ones that you've been taught to
    believed were unbecoming of you.

Go public
    with your most private thoughts
    and share yourself with the world.
    After all we have no secrets between us.
    Your eyes don't lie.
It's that look of love
    or should I say
    that look
    of
    enslaved desire.

Free yourself from yourself.

Let go.
    Don't hold back.

Let your soul leap
into my arms.

Don't be afraid,

I won't let you fall.

Your desires
are burning inside
and the passion causes,
Your heart to sweat.
I feel the drops
dripping
upon
me.
The warm drizzle,
is forming
a sensual river
that flows
before us.
A tributary that
comes from within.

Come to me
and taste
that which begins life.

Swallow,
the tension
that hinders you
from succumbing to your temptation.

Here, take
a little love
and spread it
across your fingers.

Even better,
Take
a lot of love
and spread it
all over us.

Hold it
in your palm.
Feel
how warm and moist
love is when it is
fresh.

Love must be
held gently.
If held too tight,
it swiftly evaporates.
Be calm,
and the love
will remain with you
longer.

Be still,
I have an erotic thought
on the tip of my tongue
which I must share with you.
It's an unending reflection,
so don't make any future plans.
It never occurred to you
that I could
lick a memory into your mind.

It is not
by the virtue of your
gender,
your womanhood,
that you desire this so much.

It is that your
womanhood
has not been truly
explored.

Don't act shy, timid
nor afraid
of that which
you want
to have
and
I
have to give.

Ponder this
as you battle
yourself. . .

Life is nothing
but a Collage
of all we wanted
and desired
fused with
that which we didn't
want and a
little of the
unexpected.

Allow me to
make your
Collage
from all that
you want
and I will leave
no space for the
unwanted

.

My desires
are beginning to escape me.
They're running down
my skin
and
coming together
into a basin of ecstasy.

All
that remains
is
a still-life
in our memory.

Your hesitation
has denied you
that which you know
you want.

Until
the next time that
my inner desires
rise to the surface
of my skin.

Maybe then
you and I can
take a
Voyage
through
The Uncharted.

WANTING TO. . .

I want to feel
and be felt.

I want to see
and be seen.

I want to taste
and be tasted.

I want to inhale
and be inhaled.

I want to hear
and be heard.

I want to yearn
and be yearned.

I want to be
and to have been.

I want to love
and to be loved.

I want to sex
and be sexed.

I want you
to want me
the way I
want you.

To want
and to be wanted
is this asking too much?

FOREPLAY MOREPLAY

Our lips touched and kissed
Creating a feeling of passionate bliss
My tongue entered her mouth
Then slowly moving south

Down her neck and shoulder
Licking her longer and bolder
I cautiously unbuttoned her blouse
Knowing she too, was aroused

I began sucking her breast
She, gently stroking my chest
With tenderness and care
Her moist lips kissed my ear.

Warm soft hands I felt,
As she slowly removed my belt
Pants falling to my feet
Releasing portions of my body heat

Our eyes flirting, lips locking
I removed her skirt and stockings
Next was our underwear
Standing naked, completely bare

Her desires became strong
As she stared for so long
At my pulsating erection
Pointing in her direction

I looked and sighed
Then licked between her thighs
With passions getting hot
I began licking that spot
I took her body and head
Laid them across the bed
With her legs spread
She softly said.

"With your tongue, Please mop
My body, Starting at the top
Please don't stop
Until I release the final drop"

Wet tongue and deep penetration
Giving her body erotic sensation
Moving my tongue in and then out
She began to moan, then shout

"Please make love to me"
Hands grasping my body
Fingers beginning to pinch
She asked for every inch.

Up her body I slid
She asked, I did
Giving her three inches, then four
She screamed, "I want more".

Giving her six, then seven.
She asking for more in.
Yelling forgiveness for this sin
I gave her a thrusting ten.

She then got all twelve
Every inch, she loved
We pushed and shoved
All night making love.

Collective spirits exhilarating
Intertwined bodies perspiring
The mood slowly becoming tame.
As we both pleasurably came.

COME HERE

Come here,
do you hear me?

Come here
you're not listening.

Come here,
shhh, no, come here.

Don't speak,
Just come over here
right here!
I want to see you.

Come here,
right now.

Right here.

Cum here
on me.

DESERT CANDLE

A lit candle in the midst
of the desert,

perspiring,

sweating,

dripping.
Damn
It's hot

It s-w-e-l-l-s,

    erupts,
and
    melts.

Blow it,
    Blow it,
    Blow it out!

Hot wax
    sizzles,
    drips

and
    s-t-i-c-k-s.

sweltering,
    sweating,
    scalding.

It's melting
    drip . . . drip . . . drip . . . splash

the
flame flickers . . .

Blow it,
Blow it,
Just don't let
the flame go out!

SPLISH . . . SPLASH ON MY FACE

Your lips excite me,

But that which excites me more than your lips
is the desire just to
share a moment in time with you.

Just to lie next to you on the bank of the river
of wet dreams.

Immerse myself within the stream of your love.

Splashing in the essence of your fluids,
flowing from the center of you.

Splish . . . Splash
on my face

But what excites me more

Is allowing my tongue
to stroke its' way towards the origin of that
luscious watercourse while dancing on the ripples of your
substance.

Splish . . . Splash
on my face

But what excites me more

Is swimming in your succulent juices. . .
feeling and watching the gravitational effect
pulling and pushing the tides of you.

Splish . . . Splash
on my face

But what excites me more

Is dunking myself deep down under
and when I come . . .
up for air, inhaling the aroma
emanating from that
nucleus of life.

Splish . . . Splash
on my face

What excites me more

Is barreling over the Niagara of you,
diving head first into your reservoir

Splish . . . Splash
on my face

But what excites me more
than
lying next to you,
my tongue stroking you,
swimming in you,
dunking in you,
barreling with you

Is drowning myself in your love

until my head rises
and with
my mouth wide open
I gasp
for a
taste of you.

Oh that excites me more . . .
Splish . . . Splash on my face.

HOOKIE IN JULY

A Hot July day
  we chose to play hookie
  from what I don't remember.

No electricity,
  a power outage or did the utility company receive my check?
  did I send a check?
  I don't remember.

The curtains seemed to be glued to the window
Mother Nature must have been holding her breath?
  I don't remember.

Red sirens
  screamed in the heat.
Were they on their way to put
  out the Solar fire,
  or to suppress our burning aspirations.
I don't remember.

We gasped for air
  as the youthful voices
  rejoice on the tar mat several floors below us
jubilant about being young I guess.
  I don't remember.

Popsicle sticks
  serving as tongue suppressors
  in their mouths.
Reminders of assorted sweet pleasures
  that graced their lips.
I don't remember any of flavors.

A bottle of ice water, 2 eggs,
  and a Bud were held captive by the refrigerator.

There may have been other prisoners,
        I don't remember.

Air conditioned by the waving
        of Tuesday Chronicle,
        or was it last Thursday's?
        I don't remember.

You lit a Newport,
        or a Newport Lite or was it a Kool.
        I don't remember.

Why you wanted a cigarette,
        I don't remember.
Thoughts of going outside
        sizzled in our chatter,
but we didn't go, we stayed inside.
        I don't remember why.

We made love all day
        tangled in saturated sheets,
        that straddled the floor and mattress.
        Sweating like ice sculptures on the Equator,
        splashing in warm puddles of passion,
        sharing a Bud and a Newport.

        We made love all day long
        Oh goddamn, I remember!

A NATURAL

My eyes transverse Her geography.

Exploring the contours of Her landscape,
the mountains, valleys and peaks.
All arranged into a splendid panorama.

Beauty. . . more than that. . .

The moisture interlaced with Her background,
as it streamed down the curvature
of her earthy body.

Spontaneity withheld within Her.

The natural rays touched Her exterior and
I felt the warmth of Her
golden autumn expression.

She glowed . . .

She possessed a gentle grace.
Nature's Charm.

Evolution of time
created such
a genuine splendor.

And the earth
revolved,
revolved
around this vision before me . . .

With a deep breath
I inhaled all
She had to offer.

I craved to immerse myself
between the crevasses
of Her landscape

and embrace the essence
of everything She is.

Everything Man could truly desire
originates from Her.

Beauty . . . she has more than that . . .

Underneath Her landscape,
subordinate to Her comeliness,
Man has searched for treasures.

His wealth of pleasure . . .

But deep within
the core,
the heart
lies eternal gratification.

Her reservoir of spontaneity
waiting to erupt . . .

The elements
of everything
that is and will be
lies within Her.

On my knees
with Her above me,
below me,
surrounding me,
I
Thanked God
for Her existence.

DO YOU…FEEL IT?

Do you feel it?

in this moment
        before it is spent

Listen…

Do you feel it?

My hunger for your kiss
My pain when you are missed

Do you feel it?

My lips upon yours,
        Tongue making a pass.
My warm hands grasping your ass

Do you feel it?

My moisture
between your thighs,

My lows, my highs.

My laughter, my cry.

Do you feel it?

        Whispers upon your skin,
        My love begging to get in.

Do you feel it?

My tongue wandering around
        on its way downtown.

Do you feel it?

The flesh on my face
caressing your secret place.

Do you feel it?
Your rivers cumming down,
    Me about to drown.

Do you feel it?

    My fingers dancing up your spine
    How this moment is being defined
Perpetual love
    involving your body and mine.

Do you feel it?

    You opening wide
    that sensual, romantic ride
    me cumming inside

Do you feel it?

My howls, my screams
Last night's dream
    with a theme
    of you
it always seems.

Do you feel it?

My throbbing
Heart
in your hand,
    sweat dripping from my glands.

Do you feel it?

My craving Soul
simply searching to be whole.

Do you feel it?
My words,
My thoughts,

My feelings.

Tell me,
Do you feel it?

Listen…
Do you…feel it?

WHERE IS THE LOVE?

Where is the Love?

It's right here under my nose
I breathe love.

Where is the Love?

On my lips
I taste love.

On my fingers
I touch love.

Where is the Love?

In my ears
I hear the sound of love.

I see love,
All over me
I am Love.

I am Love frontwards.

That L.O.V.E. Love
***L**ong **O**verdue **V**alentine **E**rotica*
Love
The love your heart desires
and
your mind fantasizes about.

I am Love backwards
E.V.O.L.
***E**verlasting **V**agabond **O**mnipotent **L**ove*
That powerful love that leaves you,
yet stays with you through eternity.

I am Love sideways.
O.V.L.E
I am Love upside down.
Inside Out.

I am pure love.

I am venomous love.
That poisonous love that bites you, bringing you to your knees.

I am healing love.
That sucks the pain right from your body.

I am that luscious love.
That fanatical love.
That crazy love.
That licking love.

I am that virgin love.
Pure and fresh love.

I am that parental love.
That love that makes you slap
your mother
for wanting this love.

That love that makes you
embrace your father for not
leaving you on the sheets love.

I am that fire love.
That love that makes your insides hot.

I am that religious love.
That love that makes you thankful
for being able to enjoy this love.

I quest to quench your thirst of love.

I drip love.

I live to love.
I love to live.

I am all that love
plus love.

Where is the love?

The love is here.
I AM LOVE.

FRUITY FREAK

My Fruity Freak
Can I get a sneak peek?
At your Cherry.
You don't have to sugar-coat it,
I'll eat it anyway.

Let your peach fuzz tongue-tie
My
Desire to place my seed inside ya.
You know,
You can't reap what you don't sow.
Nothing fertilized, nothing will grow.

Anyway, I prefer to lick you like a sweet, wet honey-dew melon.
I just want to experience the honeyed juices coming.
Blend in the COCO-NUT Soul flavors.
Delicious combination, we both crave for.

Fruity flavors of a strawberry,
Stuck inside a cherry
And Cream
Mouth-watering so it seems.
Makes you want to take a sip,
Instead flip,
Get your backside with some of my Cool-Whip.

My Fruity Freak
Can I get a sneak peek?
At your Cherry.
You don't have to sugar-coat it,
I'll eat it anyway.

Let me eat the skins,
From the apple.
Unlike Eve committing more sins
I'll eat the skin and more
Devour the apple to the core.

So do you want to lick the Bosco Banana?
Place your lips upon it, Ooo can ya?
Let your mouth wrap it tight like a small bandanna,
On a large head.
And Who said
That a Bosco Banana couldn't be red.

I'll lick and nibble on your plum.
Make fruit juices if you give me some.
I want it fresh and I want it soon,
Cause a plum is not plum once it's a prune.

My Fruity Freak
Can I get a sneak peek?
At your Cherry.
You don't have to sugar-coat it,
I'll eat it anyway.

Ooo, I have this fruity notion,
For my fingers to do a circular motion.
And gently, oh so gently persuade
Fresh lemons to make lemonade.

So my fruity freak,
Whenever you try to sneak
and eat
A fruit salad, Oh beware.
Because when you hear
That voice humming,
It's the fruit man coming.

THANK YOU

You opened wide
and allowed me to come inside.
You felt feelings
that feelings never felt.
Your complexion confessed.

And I,
covered in the essence of you
nature's fragrance,
possessed 3-D thoughts of you
desirable, delectable, delicious.

In that momentary
slice of life,
dessert for the divine,
my hunger for any and everything
was no longer.

You were everything to me.
Twice.
More than most could handle,
and too much for many to appreciate.

My memories are now
my eternal
"thank you card"
from you,

With your signature
etched in my emotions.

Until next time . . . Thank You.
P.S.
You are so fine,
I'd make love to your shadow
on a cloudy day.

MISSING YOU TOO!

The microscope in my kaleidoscope
convenes my Love on that perfect spot…
where your psychedelic prisms
take me over the rainbow to that
orgasmic place
where words well…are not needed.
Oh the smell of you
surfs my rhythmic brain waves
and my mind dances and romances
on the ocean of memories of your wetness.
The sand, warm and moist
filters through the fingers on the hands of time.
And I'm missing you.
A seashell sitting on the shore,
sipping a salt water martini
anticipating the ocean to come…
immerse,
saturate
and splash all over him
Wanting to go home together.
Missing you to say the least.
An exquisite canvas you are,
I want to stroke majestic colors
up, down, across your surface.
Let me paint inside of you.
Pose.
Take the brush, take it.
Do we have time for a mural?
Can you, will you, allow me to do you,
the way you like to be done?
Do you know that I'm missing you?

Break Up

In the youth of life
Why does a man shudder at taking a wife?
But through his life's own passage.
He finds that he fears love and not the marriage.

EVERYTHING WILL BE FINE

When I fell running as a young boy,
my mother wiped off my skinned knees
and said
"Don't shed any tears, everything will be fine".

When I fell off my bicycle
my mother had the remedy for my bruises
and said
"Don't cry, everything will be fine".

In all my mother's maternal wisdom
she never said what to do
When I fell in love
  or when my heart was broken. . .

"Don't shed any tears, everything will be fine."

<u>LATELY</u>

Lately I've been thinking of you.

Reminiscing about the times spent together.
Remembering the love we once shared
Thinking of those moments when we expressed how we cared.
Thoughts that will always remain.

Lately you've been on my mind.
Recalling those special times. . .
There was the time that...
and the time that we...
and the time you...or
how about that time that...oh that was some time we had together.

Lately I've been wondering how you were doing?

Lately I've been missing the comfort of your smile.

Lately I've been pondering the possibilities of a reunion.

But I tried to make the desire vanish.

Lately I wanted to hear your voice.
I've been wondering if I should call
But I quickly change my mind.

Lately I've been wanting to know what you're thinking about...
if I'm a segment of your thoughts.

Lately I've been thinking of you
and

Lately I've been thinking if any of this would matter to you.

WHAT DO YOU WANT... MY LOVE?

So my love, what do you want from me?
A whisper fades with the gentlest shift in the heart.
True love knows not a whisper.
So speak what you feel.
Come ...with me.
Disrobe your feelings.
Let the winds of tenderness
grace everything that you are.
Spread, Extend, and Open yourself.
Let it all in...every drop
of possibility.
Nakedness is to be open to everything.
It is the clothing of birth.
Bare the soul completely and it will keep you true.
What do you want from me my love?
The space between what you say you want and what you are afraid of getting narrows.
Paradoxical to say the least.
You want love...my love?
Interesting.
Do you really want...my love?
For to have it is to risk losing it.
Experience love and you may experience the inexperience of love
That frightens you...because it hurts.
Oh the space narrows.
So do you want my love?
Hear the Gods speak...
Touch and smell the petal of the flower.
Today it is soft and vibrant.
Tomorrow or the next it shall fall to the ground wilted and dry.
Dead, one may say or just a different form of what it was on a yesterday.
But today it is love in the purest.
And you have experienced a touch of that love.
To not experience it will not prevent it from dying tomorrow.
It only prevents you from experiencing love today.
To refuse to touch it doesn't change it.

It changes you.
Are you waiting for the flower to bloom before you touch it?
Listen when I say that it is a touch that makes the flower bloom.
The concern should never be on the death of the petal tomorrow
but on the death of your heart today.
So I ask again, what do you want from me?
The space between what you say you want and what you are afraid of getting narrows.
You want my love?
My love has always been there.
It is you that hasn't…
My Love.

GIVING

I wanted to give you everything

that the world had to offer.

I failed to give the most precious gift

one can give...

The gift of oneself.

A DESIRE TO KNOW

Desiring To Know

I want to know
where the wind begins
and the universe ends.

Maybe, where the sun goes
when it dips beyond
the horizon.

I want to know
where yesterday disappeared to
and if tomorrow will emerge.

I want to know
why the moon follows
me on a soft summer night
or why the stars hide
in the daylight.

Subtle questions for poetic scholars.

But nothing seduces my curiosity
as much
as yearning to know. . .

Do you still love me?

IF I TOLD YOU

If I told you that I love you,
would you care?

If I told you that nothing mattered without you,
would you respond?

If I told you, you were the most important thing to me,
would you hear me?

If I told you I give my life for you,
would it matter?

You answer yes. . .

Then I ask you,
Why do you keep fucking up?

LOOKING FOR LOVE

In all the wrong faces.

Let me try to understand
your desire to have a Man
or more importantly to have a ring
    on your hand.
Yet in the midst of
    a conversation
is the revelation
of your philosophy
    for retaliation
    that now I'm able to see
which is to give away the pu…
To another male,
    who steps to you
    with some half-ass
stale
    bugaloo bullshit
that ought to be in braille
    because evidently you are blind
to the kind
    of love that has my heart intertwined.

Looking for love in all the wrong faces.
Looking for love in all the wrong faces.

I try to stay in sync
but I am on the brink
of destruction
from your rhythmic melodic
    psychotic
mood swings
that you call love.

You exist in a duality of
your reality
that has created a state
of confusion.
Was it a likely fate
that this would all become an illusion?
You step to me with that
"babbling barrage of belittling bullshit"
that I just cannot get with
anymore,
so when I step through threshold
of today into tomorrow
and there is no sorrow
on my face
because I refused to borrow
what I thought was mine in the first place.

Looking for Love in all the wrong places.
Looking for Love in all the wrong places.
The persistence of your existence
is based on being with another,
that now you will accept any brother
that will have the right line, time, or rhyme
in his repertoire.
Do you even know who you are?

SO LONG

Now we're upon this moment,
Our time has been spent,
And though many may say it's wrong.
It is time for me to say, "So Long".

Things are not like they used to be.
The love is gone between you and me.
My mind can no longer take the strain.
My heart can no longer feel the pain.
We once fit like a hand in a glove.
Now all we do is push and shove.
Joy filled our days and happiness our nights.
Now we just argue, fuss and fight.

I know it is now time for me to move on.
To go and start over by myself, all alone.
My heart and mind tell me this is a must.
There is nothing left between us.

Over and Over and Over I tried.
Each time you hurt me, I could have cried.
But I had to be strong.
Now I have the strength to say, "So Long".

You say, you want the relationship to be right.
But when I asked to make love to you at night,
You act as if you don't have a clue.
So, what do you expect me to do?

I know you never ever believed,
That one day, I would have the courage to leave.
But you've done me so wrong.
It's time for me to say, "So Long".

Playing games with me got you nowhere.
Baby just see how you like playing solitaire.
You never will understand,
When you've been dealt a winning hand.

No longer will I beg for your love and affection,
Only to have to feel your rejection.
We played as a duet, one or more times a trio.
But guess what, I'm now playing solo.

Now the moment is here.
Let's not waste any tears.
You are now all alone.
It's time for me to say, "So Long".

ANOTHER TIME

If I could reverse the rotation of this world,
and take us back to the first day we met.
My arms would reach out and curl
around you. Our past we would forget.
All your worries you could let go
and every doubt replace with a 'know'.

If I could change the spin of this earth
and take us back in time.
I would prove your value and your worth.
You would have more reasons than rhymes
to tell you how much I loved you.
There would be nothing I wouldn't do.

I would change every tear of pain
into rivers of joy.
My love would be free to be insane.
Each moment would be one to enjoy.

I would right every wrong.
Each dark moment would be filled with light.
Every poem would become a song.
And I would commit to every 'might'.
Our days will be filled with romance,
and our love wouldn't rely on taking a chance.

If I could take us back in time,
I would love you completely.
You would know that you were mine.
We would have the love that was meant to be.
My today would be different.
I would have not failed on our commitment.

If I could just have that moment back again,
I would do things a more loving way.
My heart would be totally in.
I would hear every word you say.
If God allowed me to go back in time,
without hesitation I would make you mine.

If I could just have that moment back again,
another opportunity to begin.
To renew what has now come to an end.
I would make you my lover and my friend.

A SPECIAL PLACE IN MY HEART

I've dealt with the misery and strife.
Since the night I let you walk out of my life.
Many times I asked myself, "Why?"
We let the years roll by.
When we both knew, what could have been.
So, I asked you, "Can we try again?"
If given one wish, it would simply be,
For you to know how much you mean to me.
Now I know, from you I will never part.
For you there remains, "A Special Place in My Heart".

Though I could not express these words to you,
Please believe me, they are sincere and true.
And I will always hope and pray,
That you too feel the same way.
As we wonder what the future may hold
I will always remember what I was told
"Together the world could have been ours",
I say, "Including the heaven and stars".
Nothing is important to acquire.
When it is you that I desire.
If that one wish would come to be,
Forever I would make you want me.
Never again will you depart.
Now you know you have, "A Special Place in My Heart".

THE WELL IS DRY

Overcome by the thirst for you,
On my knees, I tried to sip from your Well
With tears in my eyes,
I realized that the Well was dry.

When the Heaven's cry my cry,
With delicate teardrops,
And the thirst for you has not diminished,
I will savor the taste, for God had the Well replenished.

THE SOUND OF SILENCE

The blaring sound
of unwelcome Silence
deafens the spirits.

There is no serenity
in the tranquility of
loneliness.

With you,

I
could hear,

The sunrise as
as it brushed
against the edge of the world.

I
could hear,

The blades of grass
conversing with each other
when the wind blows.

With you,

I
could hear the water dripping
at the bottom of the ocean.

With you,
I
could hear,
the words from your love letter
as it twirled in blustery weather.

But since you've been gone
All I hear is the deafening sound of silence.

WALK TOWARD THE MOON

Walk toward the moon,

There I'll be,

Waiting,
Anticipating,

sitting on the shore under the heavens

to be with you again.

My heart is open, so you can step right in
and we can dance with love on the ocean.

We were who we were
when we were
together.
Some say it's rare
When you care for another

the way I care for you as a friend and a lover.

I am just a man
On my knees in the sand

with empty hands.

No longer able to hold the woman

that I love.

Walk toward the moon

There I'll be

Waiting
Anticipating

sitting on the shore under the heavens

to be with you again.

Go find what you seek
only to discover nothing new
for you'll never find another
that will love you like I do.

You're free

to swim in the sea
of your new reality.

So go your way
and I'll go mine
but I will be waiting for you
where the moon shines.

At midnight

when the ocean sleeps with silence

and your experience
has you drowning in loneliness…

Look to the sky

Look high

for the I
in I Love You.

It will bring you to the man
kneeling in the sand.

So just…

Walk toward the moon,

There I'll be,

Waiting,
Anticipating,

sitting on the shores under the heavens

to be with you again.

IF WISHES WOULD COME TRUE

Another weekend has come and gone
Thinking of you, I sit home and alone.
Wishing you were here for another night.
So, I would have the chance again to hold you tight.
To touch your face and whisper in your ear.
Memories of the love that we share.
To look in your eyes and stroke your hair,
Then I realized that you are nowhere near.

And I sit and sit, oh so lonely.
Like the final leaf on an autumn tree.
Hoping for the wind to blow softly.
Setting me free to go wherever you may be.

I pick up the phone and press redial once again.
Hoping to hear your voice on the other end.
Saying, "Hi Honey, How are you?"
Only if my wishes would come true.

You are not there to answer the phone.
So I remain empty and so alone.
I stare into the night at the brightest star.
Wondering and wondering where you are.
Oh how I regret letting you out of my life.
Oh how I regret not making you my wife.
For only if I had another chance.
Across the threshold we would dance.
Oh how happy I'd be to be blest with you.
Only if my wishes would come true.

But I sit in my house, doing time.
Being sentenced for a love crime.
This is love's solitary confinement.
This is my punishment.
For letting you go.
When I loved you so.

Each day your love, I yearn.
Each night in my bed, I toss and turn.
Dreaming and wishing you will return.
But I wake up into a nightmare.
Looking at the empty pillow, you are not there.
So I lie in the bed all alone.
Staring at the walls, listening for the phone.
Baby, Oh how I miss you.
Only if my wishes would come true.

Next to me would be no empty space.
And on that pillow would be your face.
Only if the world knew.
How much I loved you.
Only if my wishes would come true.

Have you ever noticed that wherever Love has been something divine happens?

MOONLITE SOLITUDE

A moonlight chandelier
        hangs from a midnight ceiling.
I sit at the window
        looking out
        looking in.
You've only be gone a short time
        and already
the emptiness crowds me.
I wonder where you are,
maybe who you're with.
The time of your arrival
in my life
was all wrong,
so, I declared many times
The truth is
        it didn't matter what time the
        Love Train brought you in
        because I wasn't even at the station.
My philosophies and edicts
        didn't allow me to be there for you
        when you appeared.
All you wanted
        was to feel
        secure
        loved
        needed
        valued.
I gave you none of these.
The storm of our misunderstandings
        have moved out
        with the tides of our sensitivity.
Sometimes we can't even
        enjoy the simplicity of
        a quiet chat.
Sunrise Pleasures
are but a memory

a moment
a time,
When you and I were....in love.
What matters now
    is that you find
    happiness & joy.
My Love
    I relinquish myself
    from your life
    in the hope
    to make way for another.
I shall miss
    your touch,
    your kiss,
    your love,
    you.
In my heart
    I know you're the one.

So as the Love Train
departs
with you on board.
I
    wave,
    wipe the tears
    wonder.
Alone

Wherever your destination
    I pray
    that someone
    will be there
    at the station
    under a moonlit
summer night
    for your arrival.
You deserve that
    ....everyone does.

I

blow a kiss
in the wind
to follow you.
And in your moment
of Moonlight Solitude
when your thoughts
are of me
it will lie upon your lips.

Goodbye

My Love.

The End

Love is as the unfettered sparrow
That has been freed from its cage.
Like the feathers of Cupid's arrow
It flies into a Golden Age.

THE DANCE OF THE NAKED SOUL

Flesh to spirit we lie
amidst the soul of our relationship
that breathes unending life between us.

Our Dream sharing courts us in
this twilight hour and
visions of happiness
dance upon us.
The vividness of immortal
devotion connects us more than
the ephemeral explosion of sensuality that we often
share.

Momentary omnipotence harbors us from
the wrongs of the world and a
melodious conversation expresses itself with love
that is absent of all words.

Many times we've
encountered each other in this place
where naked souls embrace.
Love mortals know nothing of this
experience.
To say I Love You could not conjure
the depth of my emotional well that you've created.

To make love to you with words,
thoughts and deeds prior
to a flesh rendezvous will take
our mind, body and soul on an orgasmic path
that transcends our limited physical existence.
A journey to an unimaginable realm that only a
Divine pair could possibly know the way.

I enter your temple
and there at the Altar of Love
I engage in
Spiritual intercourse with you.
The gatekeeper is released from the duty
of protecting our emotional insecurity.
Light permeates our Souls
taking us to the beginning,
to the Garden.
There you and I stand as One
with the wisdom of Self
and the Voice speaks from within.

A
dialogue of Love, Eros,
begins
the mystical evolution between
binary beings
that many disavow to truly experience.

The accretion of two souls becoming One
disproves theoretical mathematics while
authenticating the Universal Law
of Love.

Divine intimacy possess everything that
We are
and
A Oneness
is created
that embodies
reality and imagination.

With you
there is no
gender separation or mental disconnection
There is no you and no me.

I willingly surrendered myself to this communion.

The essence of you is upon me
and I know Love.
With you in my life
I've come to know God.
Because of God
I've come to know you.
God and you
have brought me to this place
where
I've come to know Me.

I travel through life,
God's royal residence,
with you
as
my companion.

Our hearts marry
taking us on a migration through
eternal euphoria.

The wetness of
Heaven's
joyous tears
rain down upon the Garden
where naked souls dance.
And the flesh is nothing more
than an innocent spectator at
the ballet.

Our minds applaud the performance.

Ashes to ashes,
Dust to Dust
only
closes the curtains
on this transitory scene.

Signifying that one of us
has transverse to prepare the encore
of Divine Eternal Love.
Befitting for God's audience.

Heaven,
a place where
I say, "I Love You"
and the Universe bestows
an angelic ovation.

Heaven
a place where
naked souls dance forever.

I kneel at
the Altar of Love
in gratitude for the blessing
of the experience of you.
God's voice speaks from within
and tells me that
You
are
the
One...

That you are
the
naked
soul
I shall
dance with
forever.

ONCE BEFORE I SLEEP

Once before I sleep
Let me hold you tightly.
Take my hand and guide me to that place.
Once before I sleep
and drift off to be held by my dreams.
Look into my eyes,
Whisper to me what I need to hear
Once before I sleep
Say the words
for me to take with me.
Once before I sleep
Let me know what I need to know
So I may go.
Before I close my eyes
Let my last thought be of you.
Once before I sleep
Lay your head upon me.
Allow our feelings to come together
Don't leave and don't hold back,
I'm not ready to go yet.
Relax and whisper to me.
Yes that's it.
Say it again.
Once before I sleep.

You Can Still Smile

MARY AND JACK

Mary had a little vagina
Whose fleece was black as the night.
Mary's vagina had never been touched
And it was nice and tight.

But Jack was nimble and Jack was quick.
Jack gave Mary some slow. . . . hmmm.

Then Jack went down, to Mary's delight.
Mary enjoyed every lick and bite.
Jack was hungry so he ate and he ate
Mary couldn't hold back, she just couldn't wait.

Mary screamed, shouted rolled all around.
She whispered a moaning sound.
Mary pleaded for Jack to enter inside her.
Jack was too much into the oral encounter.

He continued to move about slowly.
Mary oh sweet little Mary was in ecstasy.
She never thought that the feeling would be so great.
Mary didn't know what it was to be ate.

Jack nibbled on her ears and pinched her nipples.
He flexed his body, and she watched his muscles ripple.
This whole thing to Mary was something new.
She had never known what it was to screw.

Mary never anticipated the feeling she had next.
Her and Jack were about to have some hot sex.
Jack rose up and went deep inside.
Mary eyes lit up and she opened wide.

This went on and on and on.
Mary thought the days had come and gone.
There was no doubt that Mary was sweatin' Jack.
It was evident from the scratches down his back.

Mary felt Jack preparing to release.
She thought that the sensation would cease.
But Jack was all into the groove.
He wasn't stopping and Mary wasn't about to disapprove.

This feeling Mary never had
For Jack was an experienced lad.
He never ever went limp.
Guess what, Mary is now a nymph.

It is absolutely no doubt
That Mary has been turned out.
If she had a choice to pick
Mary would gladly enjoy some of Jack's . . . hmmm.

Mary has a vagina, whose fleece is black as the night
It still nice, it's just not as tight.

RAP #14

(Just In Case You Haven't Seen)

Excuse me, my sweet dear.
I noticed you are alone over here.
I'm in a rush, really in a bind.
But I think you are worth a minute of my time.
I own a Porsche, Mercedes and a Lamborghini.
Darling just in case you did not see.
It is truly all about me.
I have been educated at Harvard, Yale and Stanford.
I am absolutely fabulous, Yes Lord.
With me darling, you would never be bored.
I earn annually, six figures plus.
You really should be with me, it is a must.
I know deep inside, it is I you lust.
I have a condo, house and home on the beach.
I know these things were never in your reach.
I can give much knowledge, if you let me teach.
Never again will I use public transportation.
I owe it all to my Ivy League education.
I am constantly flattered with adulation.
The reason I will never marry,
Is because there is not a woman good enough for me.
They all seem so pathetically sorry.
I enjoy nothing but the best.
Everything else I leave to the rest.
I do not deal with such trivial mess.
I am the best and you know this to be true.
I am truly an opportunity for you.
I only give this chance to a few.
Take a minute, view my resume.
This could be your lucky day.
If you would just come my way.
I own a yacht down at the dock.
My home occupies the entire block.
I am into Beethoven and Bach.
I enjoy croquet and polo.

Something you could not do, with an income so low.
I could fill your life with glee.
Darling just in case you did not see.
It is truly all about me.

.....her response

No I am not into Beethoven nor Bach.
More into Rap, Jazz and a little Rock.
Did you notice I own everything on this block?
Excuse me, but just in case you have not seen.
You, my dear, are parked in front of my limousine.
By the way, six figures is what I pay my maid to clean.

RAP #32

(Ignored Again Naturally)

Yo, Yo, You in the blue.
Yeah baby, You know I'm talking to you.
Damn, you got it goin' on.
Why you standing there all alone.
Ain't no need for ya to be lonely.
Come here, come git wit' me.
Sweet Sweet MacDaddy.
Let me give ya sometin' good.
Give you some of here daddy's wood.
Make you love a man, like you never could.
You sweet tender thing.
All you need is a one night fling.
You'll be my queen, I'll be your king.
Ain't no need to have any fear.
This is your magician, right here.
It a make all your worries disappear.
I'll lov' ya each and every way.
You know I will make your day.
Make you speechless wit' nuttin' to say.
Actin' all snobbish and high siddity.
All stuck up and shitty.
Damn girl don't be so nasty.
You know I'll love ya up and down.
Love ya all around.
This here is the best lovin' in town.
Baby I will be your last.
Just let me tap that ass.
I'll give it to ya slow, unless ya want it fast.
If I was a baker, you be my dough.
I'd roll ya, stretch ya, work ya thorough.
I'd be in that kitchen cookin', yeah you know.
If I was a doctor and you were sick.
All you'll need is a dose of my joystick.
Make you feel real good right quick.
That dress is sure nuf' fittin'.

Yeah baby your body is definitely hittin'.
No baby I ain't bullshittin'.
I'd treat you like a Charm's lollipop.
Lick you so good, you wouldn't want me to stop.
Like Maxwell, I'm Good To The Last Drop!

If I was an artist, you'd be my canvas.
I stroke ya well, with style and class.
Make Michelangelo wanna stroke that ass.
Yeah, you know you fine.
Why can't I git a bit of your time?
You afraid I'll blow your mind?
....

Excuse me sir, are you talking to me?
I was preoccupied by the man in the 560.
He seems to carry himself so respectfully.
....

I ran rap Number 32.
Right down on you.
That's the best rap there ever could be.
And you wasn't even paying attention to me.
I've been ignored again...
....

Naturally!

PoetTree

CAFE

Featuring the words of Claude Garretson

MY BELOVED

By Claude Garretson

<u>PART I</u>

O My Beloved,
My words are incapable
of fulfilling the task
of expressing my feelings
which lie within my heart.
My syllables fail to unite
to express my thoughts and dreams
that I vividly see before my mind.
Words . . . .to give breath
to one's thoughts.
O a task for only the
greatest of poets,
the poet's poet,
to undertake.

Nonetheless My Beloved
It is my duty
to try . . .

O the fear to speaketh that
which I feel towards thee. . . .
I fear not to die a hundred deaths,
nor to lie in a lion's den
whenst its' appetite is most furious.
But I fear to give voice to my own words,
fear to give life to my own dreams.
Fear to love thee. . .fear to speaketh from mine heart.

For if I shalt not fear death
and I knowest death will come to greet me
if I not tell thee what is within
than I shalt be prepared for the inevitable union.

Yet such preparation lacks me.
For in my mind 'tis no honour to die in such a manner.

To dwell on fear
is not the cure for the illness.

The secrets of my love and desire
for thee can be held captive no longer.

O 'tis sorrowful to be held prisoner,

with mine own arrogance as the gatekeeper.

My feelings shackled to my own contemptuous walls.

To live within one's own dungeon is surely to suffer unjustly.

I have waited for the day

that the walls would crumble

and my love would be set free.

Free to fly,

Free to soar,

and perch itself upon you.

The caged bird hath no melody and I knowest

that the spirit of song for thee lies within my being.

PART II

The tears that flow within, I must abide

For they have flooded my heart inside.

Have made my mind go insane.

From fear that I may not have you again.

I have forsaken self by not making thee my wife

To lose you, I pray to the Lord to taketh my life.

For 'tis I that I have dug my own grave.

The gravedigger, tis how my emotions behave.

How could thee know

what my heart doth feel

if I could not tell thee?

'Tis my breast plate's purpose to

protect me in battle?

To keep my enemies' weapons outside,

from my sacred heart

or to shelter my emotions inside

from my sacred heart.

The curse, the curse of masculinity

is to be not fearful of death

but to be fainthearted to love.

O how the mind can be

twisted. . .to die in battle 'tis an honour. . . .to live in love 'tis shameful.

My Lord God would not

have made me this way.

'Tis the doing of my fathers before me.

The courage to die 'tis not kin with the fear to live.

For the badge of courage justly belongs to the
honorable soldier of love.

O for thee to be a spectator at
mine mind's game.
Then maybe thee wouldst understand!

I have spent
many a day
with mine soul barren
and mine heart desolate
for you were not in my presence.

Mine heart was heavy
and the burden strong.
Those days need not be
no more.

My soul
once barren
shall flourish
with excitement.

My heart

once desolate

shall beat

with a victorious thunder.

It hath been written that

"Open rebuke is better than secret love."

<u>PART III</u>

O simply to be me, simply to be me.

To be a cresting wave upon the sea.

'Tis not enough if I canst be with thee.

O to be with thee, to be with thee

Gives eternal life to the wave at sea.

What joy then to simply be me.

Before thee, my heart and eyes have traveled

like a meandering river searching for the sea.

O when the sea is found, the river ceases its wandering

and the waters become one.

The river wilst never be a river again.

You My Beloved have brought
rest to my heart and mine eyes
and I shalt never be the same again.

It doth not matter that our worlds are different
for there is only one Heaven and
from that Heaven light appeared where darkness lived.

'Tis thee that is
mine heart's torch
that causes all darkness to disappear.

So My Beloved I come to you
With my heart open.
I seek your presence My Beloved.

To keep all commitments, promises
and precepts
that make us true,
is what keeps us whole.

Aren't promises the relative
of commitment.

Whether 'tis true

or not

I shall make

them both for you.

Yes My Beloved,

I promise to stay with you 'til

the hands are straight as an arrow

and the cock ushers the morning in

through 'til

the hands lie upon one another

while the moon gallantly watches.

This era shall repeat itself again

and again

and again.

And

I will be there My Beloved

until I know you have been pleased.

Then I shall repeat the pleasure.

I shall rise

for thee

in the morning.

I shall rise

for thee

in the evening.

For 'tis thee

that commands me

to rise

and when to rescind.

For when I rise

'tis to please you.

For 'tis the pleasure

of pleasing you

that pleases me.

For my life

serves no other purpose

than to fancy your pleasures

and those pleasures

I shall fancy 'til death seeks thee out.

PART IV

Yes, I seek to lie with you

in a bed of roses

and allow the

morning dew

to moisten thine temptations.

I shall lie with you

upon the lilies in the valley

or with the figs upon the mountaintop.

I shall lie with you

while the rain

rushes upon us

or lie with you

upon the fairest of days.

For neither the place

nor the climate

shall lessen my desires.

O a comfort

it would be

To have you between

mine shadow and myself.

Tis a Utopia in the morning sun.

But the soul needs

more than basking in sunshine.

O 'tis gratifying to swallow

from the chalice of your love.

And to taste your lips

is more pleasing to the mouth,

and inebriating to the palette

than the finest of wines.

O the gladness,

to place my lips

upon your nipples

those fountains

that giveth sweet nectar

from thou breast.

Yes My Beloved,
I canst deny
no more. . .
. . . the longing to savor the ambrosia of your soul.

Yes to enter
into your soul
and to share myself
with thee
would be an honour.

To place myself
or my mouth
between My Beloved's thighs. . . .
My mind is betwixt
by such a decision.

'Tis unthinkable
to believe
that either choice
would not grant my body
what it craves?

For the same tongue
with which I speaketh
shall be the same
that is used to absorb
your candied juices.

For if thine Lord God
hath created thine
passageway
for the sole
purpose of the
canal of life,
Would it not be
a tragedy?

'Tis not the birth of life
and the pleasure
of living
the same?

'Tis my birthright
to fulfill
all that My Beloved

desires.

O My Beloved

receive me.

Yes, receive me

inside yourself

many times

until thy

reservoir is dry

and my imprint is lasting.

Receive me

as thy lungs

receiveth the air

that is consumed.

For without the air

the lungs shall surely

collapse.

Conceive my love

as the seed of life

is conceived in

a mother's womb.

I betroth my
jewels unto thee
to be placed
in thy virgin chest.
Mine jewels in thou
virgin chest
will become a
treasure
of pleasure.

The heat of
a thousand suns
shall not
equate to
the passion
that I have for thee.

PART V

O to lie my head upon mine pillow at night
With hopes to dream, to dream right.
To dream 'til the morning wakes.
To dream of you for Heaven's sake.
Dreams of you are the only kind.

That wake in my sleeping mind.
To dream of the beauty possessed by thee.
Are dreams that others dream to see.
To dream of thy gracious beauty before me.
'Tis my dreams, 'tis my mind's soliloquy.

O to close my eyes, to close my eyes,
To dream with a youthful night 'til it dies.
At the dawn of a rising morrow.
For the death of night, I feel no sorrow.
For my dreams doth not end at the end of evening tide.
'Tis the birth of a new day, for my dreams to come outside.
To dream the dreams that I dream with my eyes open.
Are the dreams silently dreamt by many other men.
When the eyes are greeted with the beloved sight
Of you 'tis more pleasing than the dreams dreamt at night.

PART VI

Thy beauty
is divine artistry.
'Tis impossible for
any human to

lay responsibility upon themselves
for creating such splendor.
O to be the
privileged fabric that lies
upon thy flesh.

'Tis more
than thy beauty
that I love.
I have learned,
for experience has been my master,
That love based
on beauty
is like snow
trying to withstand
the changing seasons.
'Tis a matter
of time
that both
beauty and love
shall melt away.

I say to those
that seeketh
such a love. . . .
It will be like
searching for a
hair strand in the darkness.
Thy hands may feel for it,
and thy eyes may look for it
but neither shall find it.

But thou that
seeketh love
for inner beauty
I say too
that it is like
searching for a
hair strand in the darkness.
But what the hands cannot feel
and the eyes cannot see
the heart can surely find.

For love canst be found

by thine eyes

or thine hands.

Love as I knowest

can only be found

with thine heart.

Such a love

I have found

with you.

PART VII

To suffer an emotional relocation

to that state of insanity

often referred to as being

madly in love.

Whenst our memories

and visions are blurred

by thoughts of one another.

To be naked

as an autumn tree

But 'tis not the flesh

that feels the coldness

But 'tis the innerself
that grieves
from it nakedness
when 'tis revealed to the world.

O to be bare
to be unclothed
and alone.
What a misfortune
when the eyes are
obliged to reveal the
sadness of the heart.
I have not
suffered such a calamity.
For you have
assured your eternal love
to me and
I shall never
feel that brisk chill
from such bare exposure.

O 'tis a glory
to be madly in love.

PART VIII

O Cupid's unblinded arrow

has pierced my flesh.

'Tis no err

that I have been stricken.

Is Love blind?

I thinketh not.

Cupid's eyes did not suffer from

the darkness of a blindfold.

For he was his

own master whenst

his hand let loose of his bow.

My waiting flesh was his solitary target.

Now mine soul pours

out through my punctured flesh,

crushing the silent walls that

surround mine innerself.

My walls

are no bandage

for Cupid's wound.

To profane my wound

is to hate love,

which is to despise Cupid's purpose.

'Tis shameful to harbor hatred.

towards love for love's sake.

Love weighs heavy

upon one's heart.

'Tis a curse or a blessing

to be obliged to carry such a load?

The universe moves about me,

but I am motionless.

The stars revolve,

and the Sun sleeps and wakes

many times but

it goes unnoticed.

For the love that I have

for thee keeps like lead

in my shoes.

I canst move forward

for my heart remains

here with thee.

PART IX

Thou are a precious gem, a jewel of the Nile.

Doth many suitors may file.

All warriors of love with promises in their eyes.

But their eyes disguised their hearts' chivalrous lies.

Such false vows I doth disdain.

These warriors shalt not shield thee from love's pain.

If our love

was ever true

Then the moon

could travel

the sky

a million times

and we need

not fear.

For true love

never diminishes.

Doth thou have no

faith in the Love

between the two of us.

How canst thee have
faith in thine God
whom thou has
never witnessed?

Is not the God
that we worship
the God of Love?
Is the faith not the same?

Doth my understanding
fall short
of my expectations?

My faith
in our love
doth not
leave me
My Beloved.
Not now, not ever.

PART X

I have prayed to our Lord God,

my bruised knees are mine witnesses. . . .

O God,

I have been born with nothing but my name.
And my death may be my birth's twin.
But please Lord doth not let my life be the same.
For I have tried to live according to Thine doctrine.

O God my mouth had not the blessing of a silver spoon.
To be without such ornaments, 'tis not an affliction.
But if I shalt have to live in love's ruin,
I pray to thee, let it not be my life's crucifixion.

Have my life's habits been the door for Satan to come in?
Have I broken thou commandments, have I committed a sin?
If I have done anything that is forbidden,
O Lord, I pray to thee that I may be forgiven.
Why hast thou taken the only reason for living from me?
And please forgive me Lord for questioning Thee.

Please Lord, just doth not keep My Beloved away.

If 'tis not your will then let my pain be at ease.

For 'til I meet you on Judgement-Day.

My living shalt be as you so please.

O Lord please, please answer mine prayer.

For each and everyday, I pray on my knees.

O Lord please doth not let me live in despair.

Please O God bring My Beloved back to me.

Amen

O God forgive me for I am not done speaking with Thee.

Are not the tears in mine eyes, my quivering flesh
or the hollowness that I feel proof of my pain?

What have I done to be cursed with such panging in my spirit?

Lord, please forgive me for questioning Thee.

'Tis that I don't understand.

Is it wrong for me to desire to know mine state of being?

Are you not the God Of Love?

Have I not abided by Thee, for Thy namesake?

You allowed me to return from battle unscathed,

when I have unmercifully slain men. Taking away their obligation of any future promises.

I have made children fatherless, mother's sonless and widowed many.

Yet I have not a battle scar upon my flesh to validate mine presence there.

You have protected me when I have dishonored Thy sixth commandment.

Lord I don't understand, why am I not amongst those on death's carriage?

For I have worn death's trimmings on my body for the sole purpose to massacre the hopes and dreams of my enemy.

Lord, please forgive me for questioning Thee.

My mind hath gone mad from life's puzzle.

Whenst I surely thought I would meet Thee I was wrong.

Now my soul and life are being meticulously pricked away.

Love's death is to die from the inside, 'tis much more dreadful

than to die upon the battlefield.

What romanticism is there in death?

O what death there lies in romanticism.

To drown in one's tears or one's blood? I wouldst glady suffocate from mine own blood.

O God, plunge death's sword into my broken heart.

Slay me as I have slain others. Take all my tomorrows from me.

I beg Thee to do so.

For my life has departed. I know not where but life has left me though I live.

Am I not a shell, a corpse that moves about the living?

Some demon from hell?

The loneliness has caused me to see the vultures of death in my mind waiting to devour what shalt be left from love's ruins.

O God, inhale Your living breath that is within me.

I beg Thee to do so.

O Lord, please forgive me for my expressions.

'Tis surely because I have gone insane.

My emotions cause all logic to be taken from my behavior.

Lord, is this the price for loving well but loving wrong?

O how I am drowning in the sea of love filled with salted tears.

O God, I pray to Thee to please forgive me.

There are angels in Your Heaven above

For the stars in the night doth show it to be true.

Cast down them with their spreaded wings of love.

Let me be touched by their divine virtue.

For in the blackness of night that lies silently.

The angels sing with such sparkling delight.

I know that one of those angels is the one for me.

The one angel that can maketh my life so right.

Yes Lord, on this earth as in the Heaven above.

Lies my reason for living, my life, My Beloved.

PART XI

To be wedded to sadness, twas not the intent.

The matrimony has my Happiness bent.

Shaped to cover my grief's hide.

O to have taken Loneliness as my bride.

To have a mistress is to disobey my Lord.

Tis misery, tethered to Loneliness by the eternal chord.

For I have written my vows none the less.

The thought of joy to be adulterous with Happiness.

If my words,

thoughts or desires

are sinful

Causing my

soul to be cursed

'til eternity

than so be it.

For my innerself
is true.

To deny truth,
is it not
the greatest sin of all?

My words
are of the
truest form
for they come
from my heart
and not merely my mouth.
For where the
mouth deceives
the heart is incapable
of such mischief.

If thine heart
is a mirror
of mine

Then thou must
speaketh thine words of love
into the wind
And I shall hear your whispers
for the mouth speaks softly
but the heart bellows.

I shall wait
many daybreaks
for the winds
to press upon my ears.
And I shall wait
many nightfalls
to press upon you.
And when
the winds speaketh
for thine heart.
I pray that which
I hear shall be that
thou loveth me
the same as I loveth thee.
With all thine heart
and all thine soul.

Then will I send

my Chariots

with all of my

horses hitched.

And I wilst

retrieve you

from thy present place.

O a sight

for mine eyes

to behold

when the moment

and thee are together.

And we shalt seek

all that is to be sought

in this life.

For 'tis life worth

living

if thou shalt

live without loving?

If perchance

death knocketh

at mine door of life,

I shalt not answer.

For there is nothing

other than our

Lord God

that shalt keep me

from My Beloved.

Signed: Your Unknown Soldier Of Eternal Love

CPSIA information can be obtained at www.ICGtesting.com
Printed in the USA
BVOW08s1941090216

436142BV00001B/3/P